UNLIKELY CHRISTIAN POETRY COLLECTION

Unlikely Christian

ISBN: 978-0-9855505-6-1

UNLIKELY CHRISTIAN

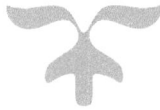

A Collection of Poetry

CHARNA AINSWORTH

Books by Charna Ainsworth

The Letter

Mountain of God

Unlikely Christian

Shades of Persuasion

Contents

Sowing Seeds..1

The Greatest..2

Fall Gently..5

When Eternity Begins...6

Heaven's Gate...7

The Son..8

The Best Is Yet To Come..10

Unlikely Christian...11

My Refuge..12

Valley of Decision...15

Leaving All...17

Who's Got My Back...18

In Darkness & In Light...20

The Question..23

Crystal Clear..25

The Day...26

Memories...29

Calling To Me...31

Remind Me...33

My Name..34

What Do You See..36

Nothing Short of a Miracle..37

Looking Up...39

Inside My Dreams...40

My Prayer...42

Patiently Waiting..44

Deep Longing...47

Direction..48

To my daughter Maria.
Thank you for the inerasable memories.

Sowing Seeds

It is a gift
these words of mine
and the way
in which they flow.
Anointed by the holy one
yes, words to help you grow.
It's faith that turns the seed
into a mighty oak tree
and faith that turns a man
into a little child again.
So these words
will go on
for generations to come
and those who read them
will see their faith grow strong.

The Greatest

How desperate I am to find the truth in Your hand…
where the nail pierce You through
where all my faith is in You.
And all I want is to adore the one my heart cries out for,
to please the one who called me friend
to bow before the only unblemished man
who took my sins far from me
and buried them in the deepest part of the sea
and forgot about what I did…
long before I became His.
Each day's journey we start anew.
He is the teacher.
I am the student of love……..
The greatest commandment of all.

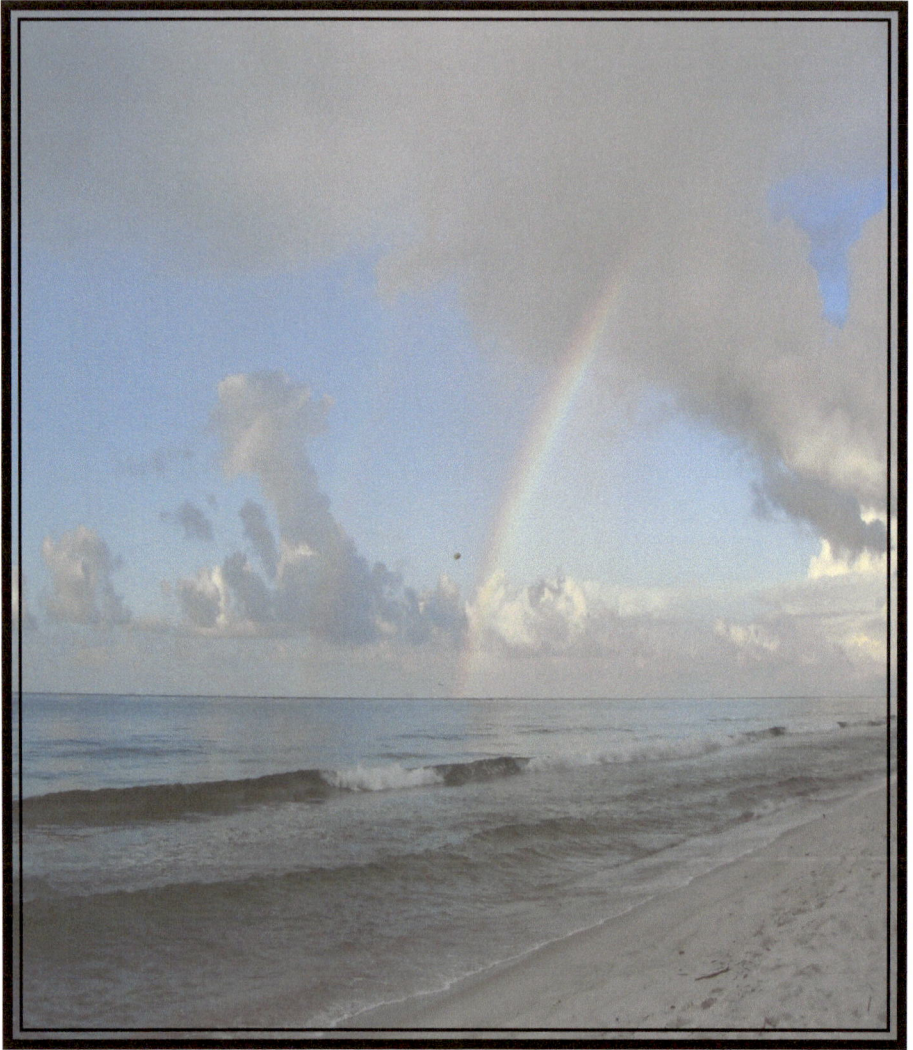

Fall Gently

I am with you to deliver you
Saith the Lord,
to be your guide and comforter
through sunny days and storms.
But if you should fall,
as most humans do
don't worry for a second;
I'll be there to catch you.
And if you should stumble,
remember my ways
and don't ever forget, my love,
there will be a judgment day.
So be like the wind
whose direction no one can know
and fall gently into the arms
that love you so.

When Eternity Begins

The ground, I once stood upon, has turned into sand.

It's shifting under this weight

that is unnatural and so profound.

I ask why?

Why is the ground so loose beneath my feet?

You answer, I'm carrying you now;

    as I cry out in disbelief.

Where is my wise counsel?

Where can wisdom be found?

I am simply…dumbfounded,

and no relief can I find.

I stood upon the words with their power and strength

and partook in the blood

and the bread I did eat.

So I ask… why does this burden feel so heavy?

You say I will understand when we begin eternity.

Heaven's Gate

Don't cry for me
I've gone to my eternal home,
my soul is at peace…
let yours be too.
Don't weep,
please just find the truth.
Then you and I will remain
the apple of God's eye;
Then the veil that separates
will be as thin as your last breath
and when you arrive at heaven's gate
all of heaven will celebrate
for a life well-lived
where we'll spend an eternity
bathed in God's holy presence.

The Son

Silent rainbows
stream across the sky
speaking of a promise
from the only one on high.
We struggle with the days
and sleep the nights away,
only to awake with blessings and grace
from the only one on high.
Soothing rain falls from a blue sky
telling us of a future
with the only one on high.
We fumble through our lives
and awake deep in the night
only to find we needn't worry or cry
because we are always with
the only one on high.

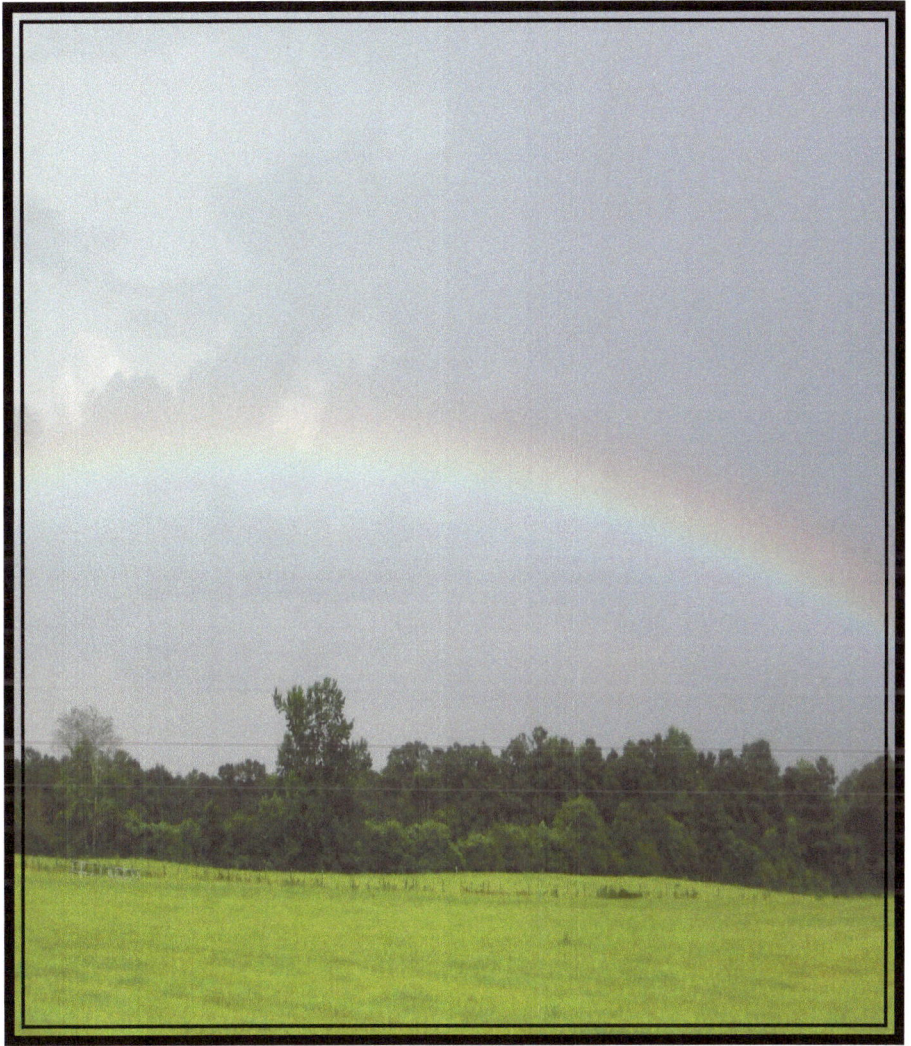

The Best Is Yet To Come

I prayed unto the Lord

and He inclined His ear.

He said, I'm listening my child.

I replied, I don't want to speak Lord, I want to hear.

I want to hear how things are going to get better.

I want to hear about 'the good life'.

You see, I feel I've been cheated with a life full of strife.

I know I've been needing too much for too long

and if You speak it then finally good would be done…

unto me; because I've been trying

my best for so long

and I speak of Your glory

and of heaven and Your righteous son.

Now, Lord, I know You're listening

so please tell me when will the bad days be done?

Yes, I know, You keep telling me

the best is yet to come.

Unlikely Christian

It's very unlikely that I would be here
so close to my Lord without doubt and fear.
The years so deeply spun with sin,
the drinking, the drugs and all the men.
I've cursed and fought with the best of them
and only had drunkards and losers as friends.
To church; what church? I'd rarely been,
but still Jesus wanted me even back then.
Year after year He'd whisper my name
but I was still busy playing 'The World's Game'.
Little by little, He captured my heart
and now there's no one who can keep us apart.
We are one, the fruit bearing branch
and the life giving vine
and He's forgotten about all those sins of mine.
I'm an Unlikely Christian in everyone's eyes
except for Jesus, who was with me all the time.

My Refuge

This is a house where never was a hand,
no hammers, no nails but secure, I am.
There are no walls or floors, or doors
but I am safe, forevermore.
Prayer after prayer went up
for something so sublime.
Yet it is a building unseen
like a fortress, held only in my mind.
Fear? What fear?
What do I have to be afraid of?
This building will never collapse
for it was built on Love.
Thankful and grateful is all that I feel
for You, my Lord are the only one
who shelters, restores and heals.

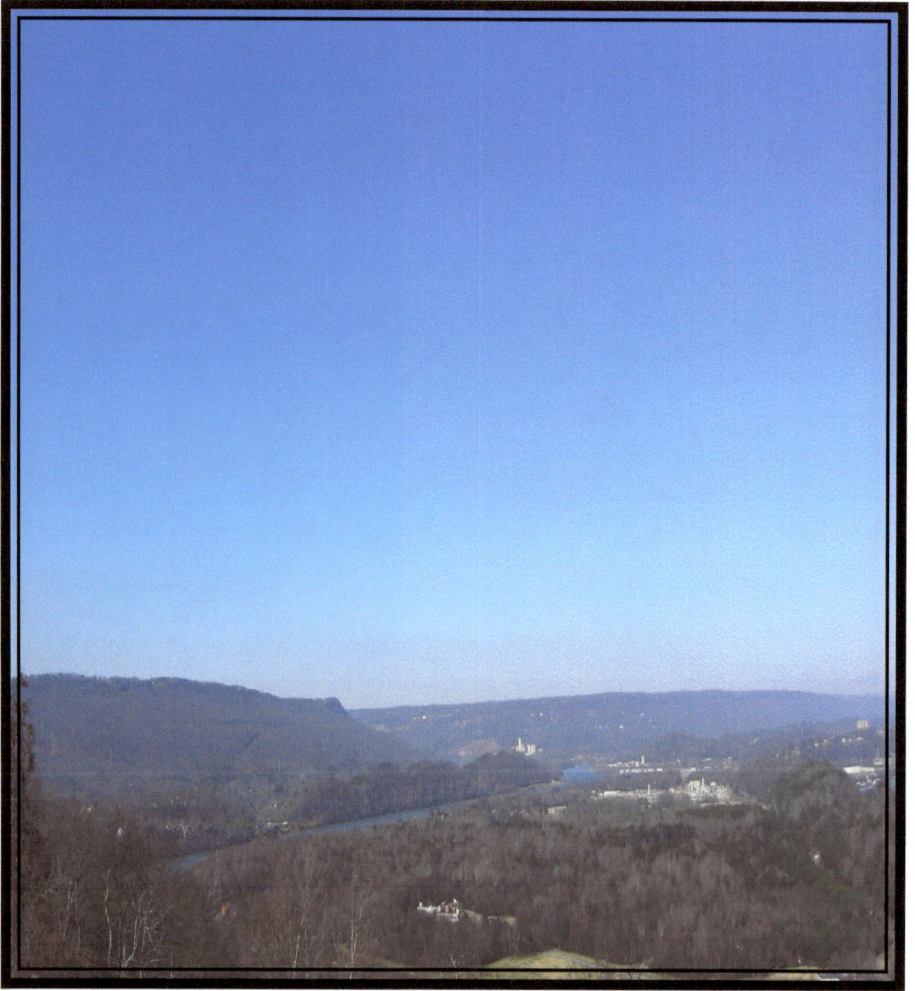

Valley of Decision

Where are you going little one?

Why do you stay?

Give Me your hand,

I'll lead you out of here, it's the right way.

Why are you taking so long to decide?

Haven't you always felt My presence

when the storms suddenly subside?

Why are you waiting; for the time is at hand.

I hoped you would be coming.

I have loved you as a child and a friend.

Call on My name, before it's too late.

The valley of decision is deep; but not too deep for Me

to deliver you from the depths of this world,

no matter the crime, addiction

or sickness you have endured.

I paid for it all; see the scars on My hands.

All I need is your answer, then I can give the command.

Go, get My child, bring them here to Me.

They have made the right decision,

now I can set them free.

Leaving All

I'm following Your lead, where ever it may go
and tho' I be afraid I will carry on and be strong.
This path is quickly narrowing… there's too much overgrowth
but ahead I see a clearing and I don't have far to go.
I'm following Your lead, Lord
please tell me what You know.
Sometimes it feels like a death-trap,
almost like my heart will explode.
My steps, at times, get a little weary
until I feel Your hand reach out and I can almost feel eternity
then I have to turn and shout
I'm following Your lead, Jesus
Cause You've called me by name.
Tho' the way seems long, I'm still moving on, day by day.
And when the journey's over…
the moment my new life has begun
I won't regret a moment
Because God's will has been done.

Who's Got My Back

Now is the time for me to be strong
and no matter what I do it can't all be wrong.
So I'm begging for mercy because it's all I can do.
But who's got my back now?
Look Jesus, it's You.
If I have to be stronger… take me by the hand
and lead me in a plain path.
Show me the way, I'd do just about anything,
because it's all I can do.
But who's got my back now?
Look Jesus, it's You.
If you can make me stronger; I think I could stay
but if You leave, I know I'll go astray.
Take me with You, on to a brighter day
where Your strength will save me and I'll be on my way
because it's all I can do.
But who's got my back now?
Look, Jesus it's You.

In Darkness & In Light

A tale of two

from one grows hope; the other death spews.

Constantly in battle

the one strikes a blow

as the other holds His ground

knowing it was never suppose to be the tale.

Envy caused this strife

and envy will end it all

the everything we've come

to know and love in this life.

How marvelous it might be

if he'd kept his heart pure

and if one could be sure

that angels do in fact

have a heart that could be pure.

Then the way of the one that divides

would perish from our minds

like a hideous gift

sent back by the receiver.

The one being day
the other being night.
Why should they fight
for a soul such as I?
A feeble fool could plainly see
that this world continually divides me
from reality on to stranger shores
where ghost are holy and Christ lives forevermore.
Tiny miracles lead up to the best
that is coming with the rest
as do the valleys with the hills.
Why such a jagged pill and why so hard to swallow?
In fact, we just want to get it right.
Righteousness is the total of what we seek
and if not for the battle
the choice would be easy.

The Question

Listen to your heart and it will tell a tale

that's certain to amuse and sometimes confuse

    even the strongest soul around.

When you feel it's beating, its' constant rhythm pound

then you will know you're living in this world without bounds.

One day, too soon, its' work will end… never to beat again.

Then your soul will fly to a brand new place

where time will mean nothing, forevermore.

There, the judge will come to hear your case.

There, the judge who rightly judges will ultimately decide your

fate.

Did you believe in the Begotten Son

or did you make fun of those who did?

Did you love and not hate?

These answers will determine your souls' fate.

Did you cry and mourn at the thought of His thorns?

Or did you turn your back when people talked about that?

Were you running toward The Door,

kneeling before the only one who could grant you grace?

Or were you running one hundred miles per hour the wrong

way?

Were you running with the wrong crowd
because your soul was too proud to admit your weaknesses?
Still the question remains,
when your heart has finally sang its final good-bye
will the judge be inclined to invite you into paradise?

Crystal Clear

The day has dawned,

I think of You beside a stream

of pure water…   waiting for me.

And I'm waiting on You

to carry me through the storm

on to a brighter day; away from harm.

A place where the past…

seems a million miles away.

You place Your hand…

   into the clear running stream

and I begin to dream of being one with You.

The day has dawned and I have cried…

   longing to be at Your side;

   has broken all of my pride.

And I am simple now,

not wanting to hide

from the deep love I'll find

the moment I look into Your eyes.

The Day

And the Lord's promise
   is like a rock.
One you would kneel in front of
   to pray.
And someday I see myself…
   all meek and mild
because I wasn't crushed by it,
just steadied myself upon
   it's weight.
And one day,
I'll think back
   to the day it was over;
then I'll lean back upon that Rock,
content just to stare into the heavens.

Memories

Does God put memories in our heart?
Why do some things seem so familiar?
Does He want us to know
we're not set too far apart from Him?
And if we tried with all our might,
could we get it…right?
Have you ever looked into
someone's eyes
and felt you've known them
all your life,
and maybe more?
How could this be the end?
Didn't Jesus say He was
a friend?
And didn't He say He'd see
us again?
Did God put memories
in my heart?

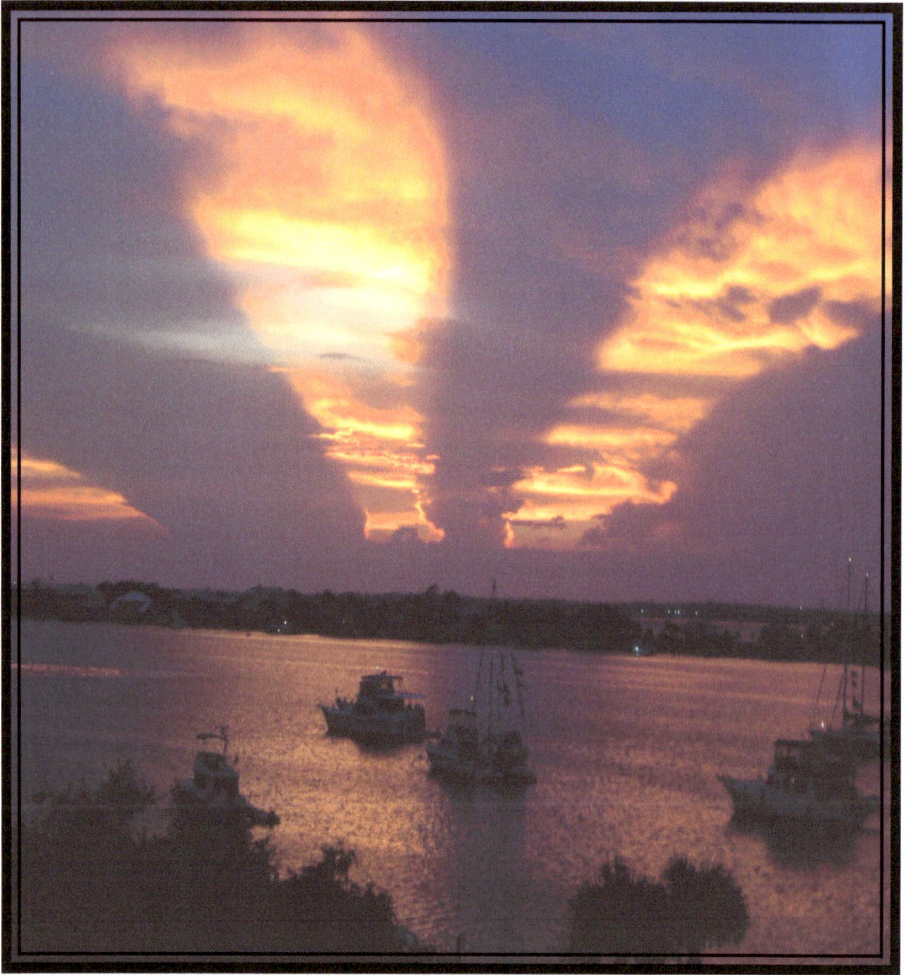

Calling To Me

I can feel it now,
so close to my dreams,
coming to light right before
my very eyes.
It's You, only You
that gives me a life,
air to breathe inside
and love like I've never known.
Here it is now,
finally, I love You completely
and Your words are my
salvation, unbelievably everlasting.
The reality of my heart,
slowly but surely opening.
Now is the time.
the truth is undeniable.

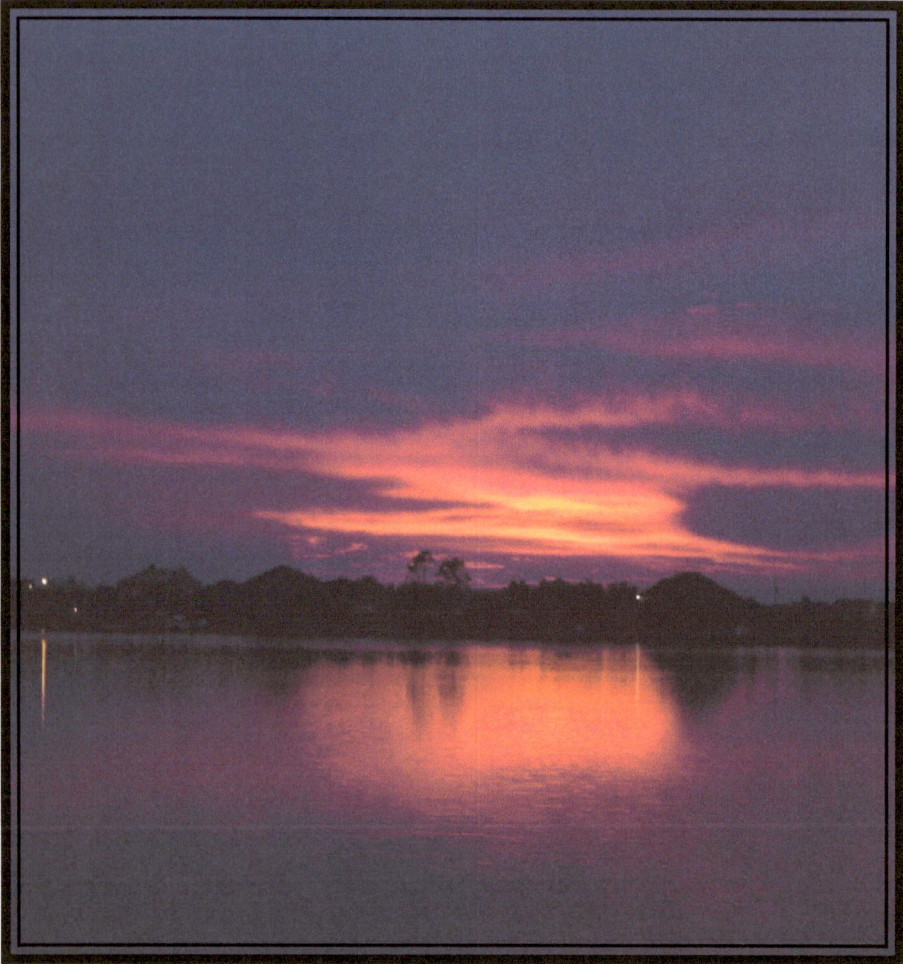

Remind Me

When night falls and I feel so alone
I come to You on bended knee…
Calling out the way I want things to be.
That I'd be whole; fresh and alive
full of the promises shared only between You and I.
But the darkness makes me look back
to a desolate sea of past mistakes…
that separated You and me.
Those complex lies take hold
with such fear…
    that I almost forget…
the promises I could once hear.
When the day arises
and I feel You with me
I come to You…
    on bended knee…
and You remind me, the past is long gone.
Only the future remains… and I must stay strong.

My Name

What do I have to fear
from a world that calls me
by a name I'd rather not hear.
It's Your voice
that truly calls my name
it sounds so sweet
to hear You say
my daughter I have great plans
for you
plans for a future
that you can surely behold
as though the tale is being told
just a story
as old as the scroll
that only knows truth
and the plans You have for me
are as awesome as the seed
of a beautiful oak tree
planted by a stream

yet it's only a dream
to me
that I will certainly see
if the path continues to lead
me on to the moment
I've been counting on
for so very long
the still small voice
that calls me queen
and knows my dreams
only because You put them
in my heart
so very long ago
before the day I was formed
out of Your love for me.

What Do You See

Look at me, Jesus.

Tell me… what do You see?

I've never been a scholar

but I've prayed for wisdom

and asked You for clarity.

I still wonder what you see, Jesus

when you look at my life.

I've tried to be giving and often avoided strife.

I believe You're my savior,

God's only son, the holy one, Christ.

But how do you see me, Jesus?

Is it the way I am?

I fall short of the glory time and time again.

It's not from lack of trying.

By-the-way… does trying count?

Please tell me what You see in me, Jesus.

And do I have to wait

    until I reach those pearly gates to find out?

Nothing Short of a Miracle

You are there in heaven sitting upon Your throne

and nothing short of a miracle

has brought me back home.

The crowd is dense… maybe a half a mile or more,

all worshiping the one I adore.

My heart wants to run

and push my way through the crowd

my feet won't move, as my knees hit the ground.

The light from Your body glows all the way to me.

I close my eyes, laying down

then stretch my arms out in front of me.

My worship goes on for hours it seems.

I do not feel worthy of coming any closer to my king.

As the wounds of my soul are closing up, I begin to feel whole.

And as I look up there's a hand stretched out;

it helps to lift me off the ground.

You carry me and sit me down

on the steps of Your throne.

Nothing short of a miracle has brought me back home.

Looking Up

Just a grain falls betwixt the cracks,

a lesson unlearned

a tragic matter of fact that led a broken girl

to find a new home

where twisted metal and broken glass

left on the uneven ground

lay under gentle bare feet that trusts and hopes

    in bigger and better things.

It was just wood, gravity and wind.

Life would never be the same again.

The future opened up and the best was yet to come.

Eyes wide open as the window in heaven swung.

The cup; so heavy… spills from the edge.

The prayers once inside

fly free from my head

to please and be hidden under the wing

is the joy the singers sing about

and prayers' pray for more than anything.

Inside My Dreams

If I believe

    and plan to achieve and have no doubts,

    it will all happen in time.

If I believe

    He is watching over me then what can be

    is all inside my dreams.

If I believe

    there's more than we see and trust my heart,

    everything will be renewed.

If I believe

    today is not too late the vision is on its way,

    then hope will be worthwhile.

If I believe

    that good things do happen to those who choose right,

    my dreams shall soon be truth.

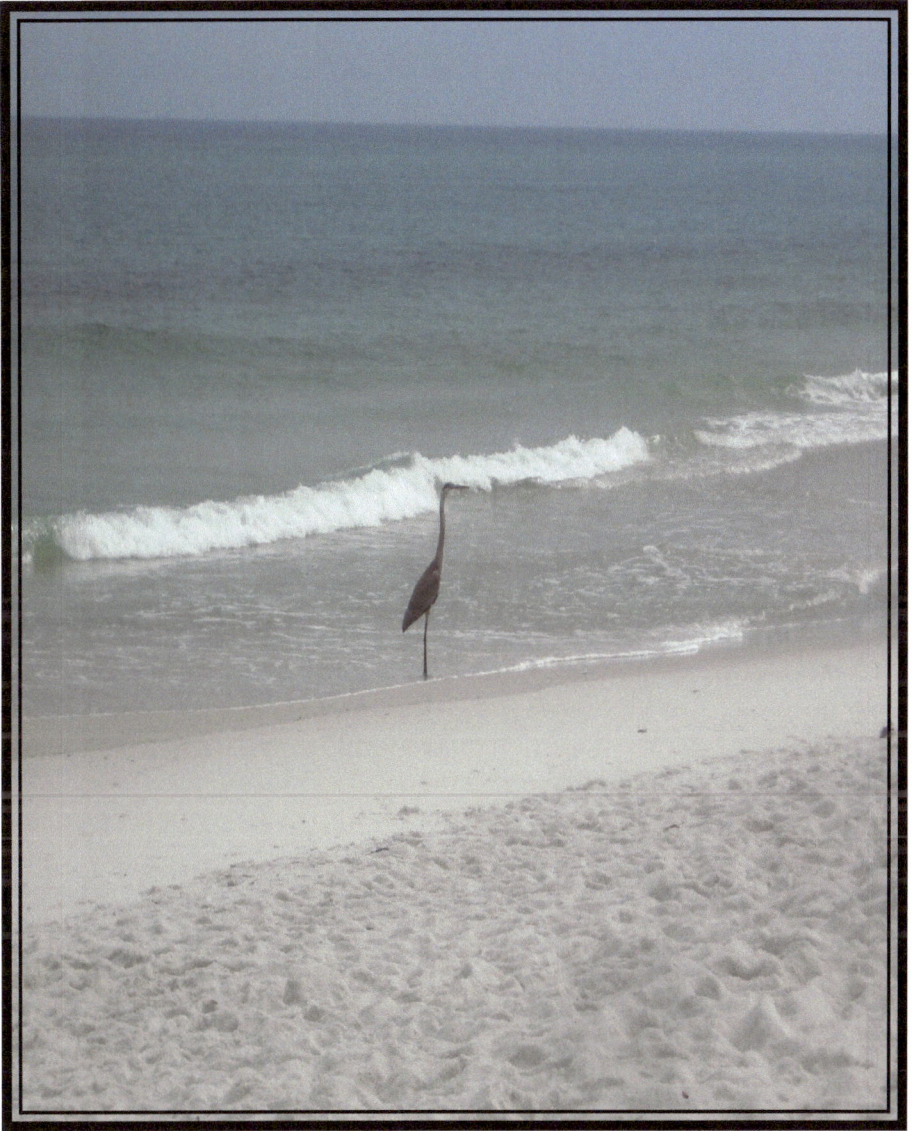

My Prayer

Let me seek You in all of my ways.

Let me find You a little more each day.

Vowing in this moment to never fall away.

Refusing to ever debate that I could be led astray.

I am the tree…   planted by the water's edge,

growing in wisdom and understanding,

as I eat my daily bread.

And the search will go on, each day, after I rise.

How can I please my Father?

What will I see more clearly

looking through His eyes?

How can He use my hands

to do His most important work?

How can my feet be His,

ready if needed to walk this earth?

Please, let me seek You, all of my days.

Let me comfort the poor, shelter the widow

and give water to those who thirst today.

Patiently Waiting

Forever, my love,
do you know what that means?
Love is waiting quietly,
sitting beside the brook,
with not a tear in His eye,
If you'll take a second look…
love waits so patently
with so few words to say,
while we wrestle with the days;
waiting, for Love to take us away…

Deep Longing

From my heart… flows the words
that cannot escape my lips.
What purpose would they find
in a world like this?
It speaks in a language
that few can understand.
They speak of a love
from the only virtuous man.
I cannot forget what He has done for me
my need to describe His truth will set me free.
Where are the others who long for Him like me?
I want to give my testimony to these;
only solitude is the barrier
between them and me.
One day I will send these words adrift in a sea
and perhaps see my gift
floating back to me.

Direction

I don't want to fad away
so this vow I certainly make
to start the day off fresh and new
and never go back to what
    I use to do
I'll look toward a future
    that is certain to be bright
and leave the addictions and
    sickness far behind.
The path will be paid for,
    of course
the blood will not be my own
and when my journey's done
this path will lead me home.

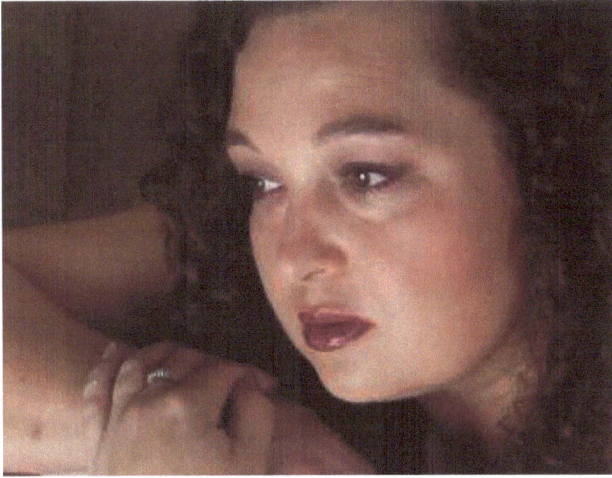

About the Author

Charna Ainsworth is an award-winning poet and the author of *The Letter*, *Shades of Persuasion*, *Mountain of God*, and *Unlikely Christian Poetry Collection*. She lives in a small southern town in Mississippi with her daughter.

Website: www.charnaainsworth.com

Follow: www.twitter.com/charnaainsworth

Friend: www.facebook.com/charnaainsworth

Watch: www.youtube.com/user/charnaainsworth

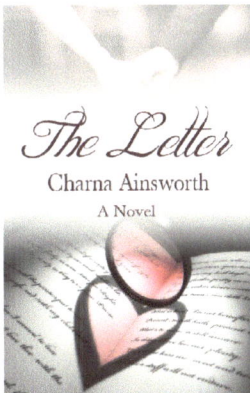

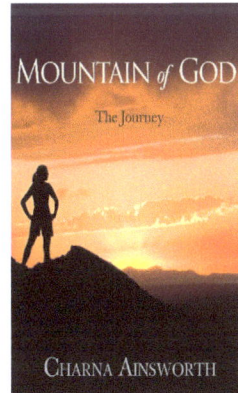

www.ingramcontent.com/pod-product-compliance
Lightning Source LLC
LaVergne TN
LVHW010027070426
835510LV00001B/10